I Am the Ocean

I Am the Ocean

By Suzanna Marshak
Illustrated by James Endicott

Arcade Publishing | New York

Little, Brown and Company

I am the ocean.
I made the beaches,
grinding stones into sand
for millions of years.
Once I wet the toes of dinosaurs,
but that was long ago.

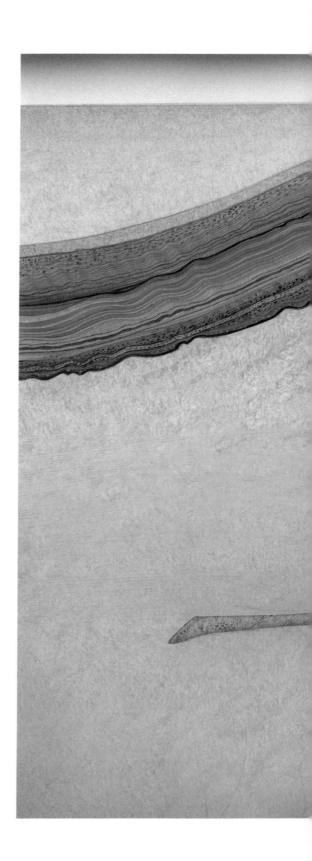

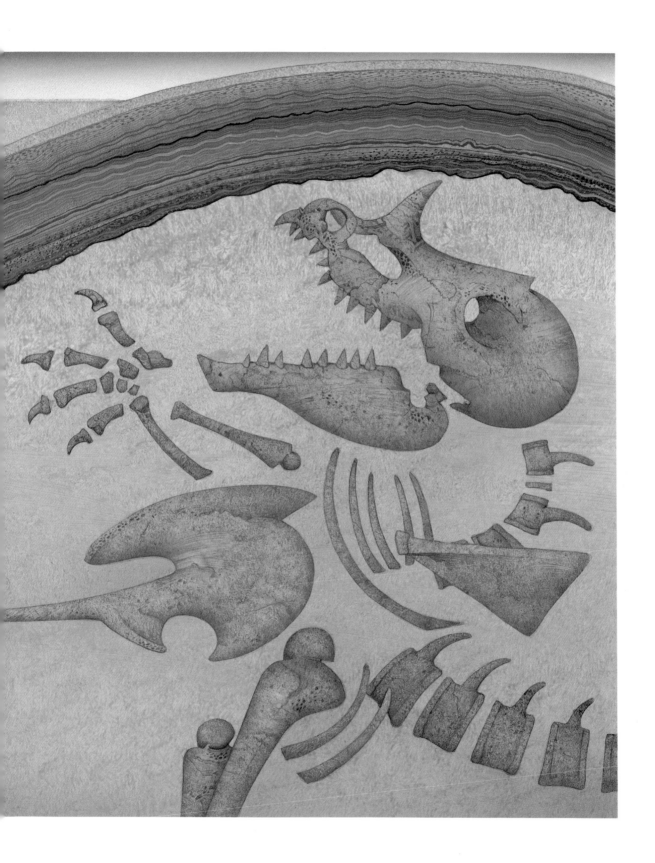

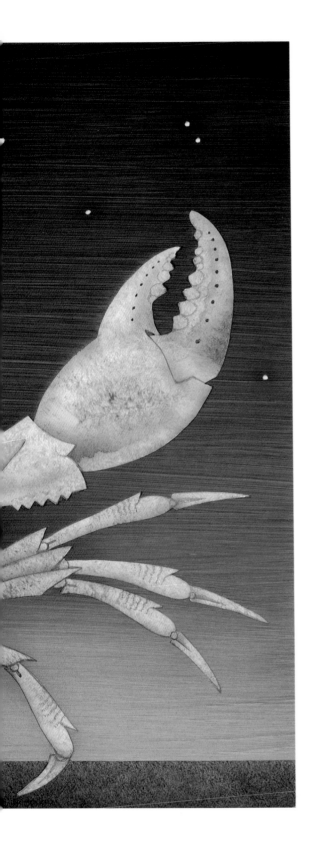

I am the ocean.
I dance with the moon.
I never change partners
and I never miss a step.
As the tides rise and fall,
the moon and I will waltz forever
on the shore.

I am the ocean.
Sometimes I am smooth and calm.
Then men launch boats upon me
to sail with the breeze.

Early in the morning,
the first sunlight slips over
my vast gray waters.

The gray turns to blue,
and blue waves crash
foaming white on the sand.

When night falls,
moonbeams flash phantom diamonds
across my deep.

High above, stars twinkle
and show ship captains
the way through the night.

Far below, other kinds of stars
walk the floor on thousands of tiny
sucker feet, looking for oysters to eat.

I am the ocean,
home to many creatures.
One drop of my water
holds animals too tiny to see.

Deep down,
shrimps glide over sea anemones
that blossom like flowers.

Jellyfish whoosh along,
opening and closing
their soft umbrellas,
glowing like parts of neon signs.

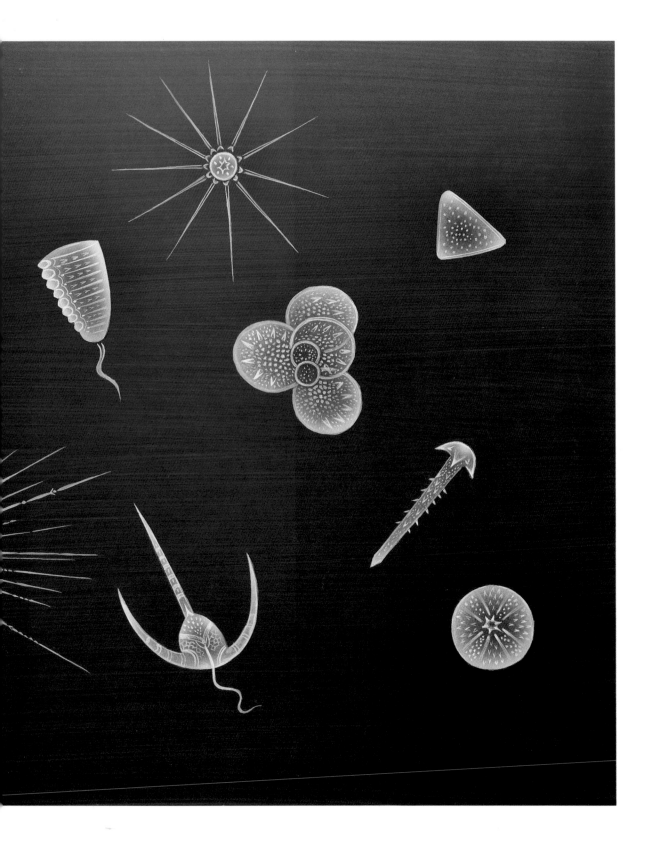

Where the water is as cold as ice,
penguins swim like torpedoes,
and polar bears hitch rides
on ice floes.

Where the water is warm,
tiny corals build reefs
that turn into islands.

Dolphins romp through the waves,
talking in clicks and whistles.
Sharks prowl and show their teeth.
And whales slap their mighty tails
upon my waters,
calling to each other
on their way to winter playgrounds.

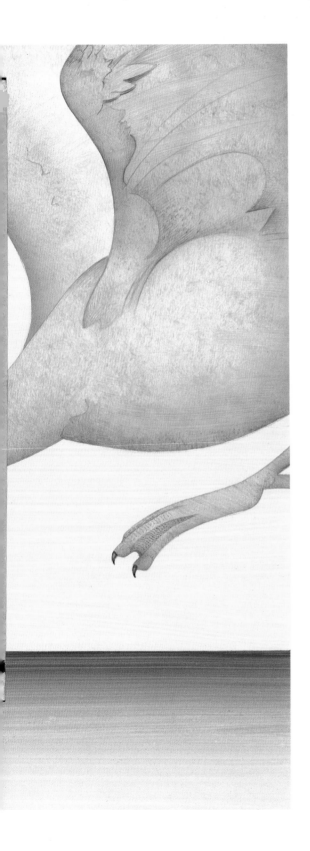

I am the ocean.
I feed the birds.

Lines of pelicans
skim low over the breakers
and dive quick for bonito.

Cormorants with sharp eyes
and long necks snatch tasty anchovies
out of my dark waters.

I am the ocean.
I am strong.

At the close of a summer day,
I tear down all the sand castles on the
beach and leave it smooth.

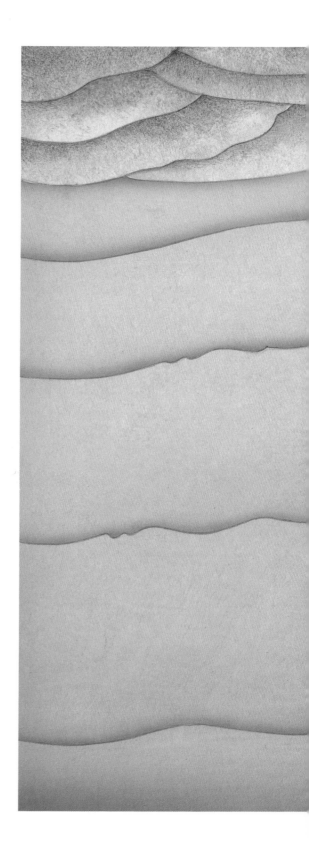

Under the shining sun,
I give up some water for rain clouds,
but I stay strong
because all the rivers of the earth
flow down to me again.

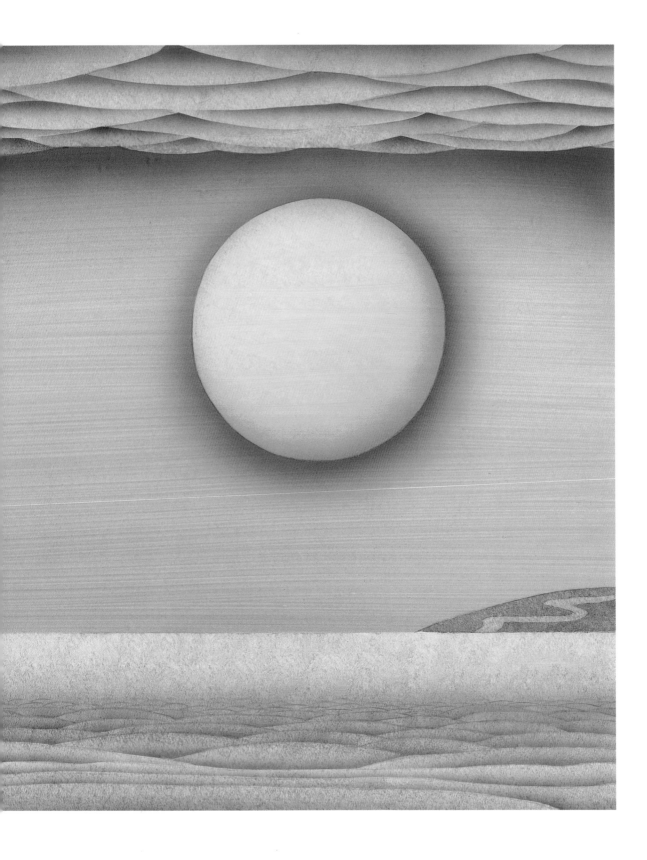

Sometimes I am not calm at all.
When dark storm clouds gather,
the birds look for trees on the shore,
and the sailors go home.

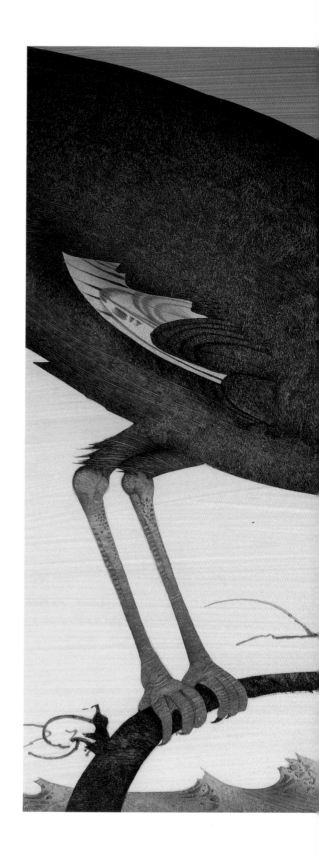

I am the ocean.

When I am angry I fight with the wind.

It blows hard

and my waves rise up like mountains.

All night the wind and I do battle.

Thunder cracks and waterspouts fly.

The strong pull of giant waves

rattles the wrecks of pirate ships,

and doubloons spill out

of treasure chests.

Storm waves catch the secrets of the sea.

They rake the bottom

and pound the shore,

over and over and over.

At last the wind grows tired.
Now the gale force dies down
to a soft breeze.
My waters grow quiet
and I rock the fish to sleep.

Once more, gentle waves lap the shore.

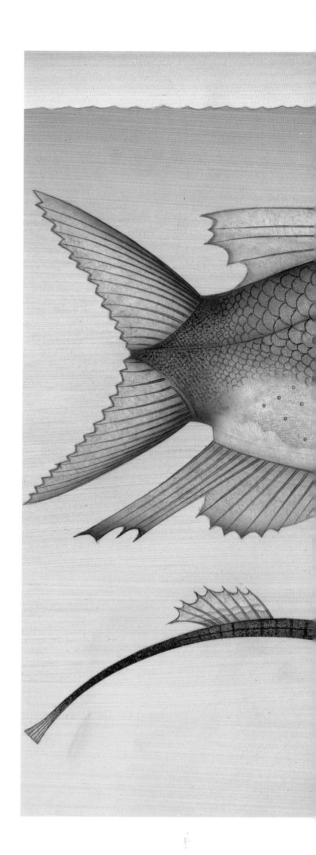

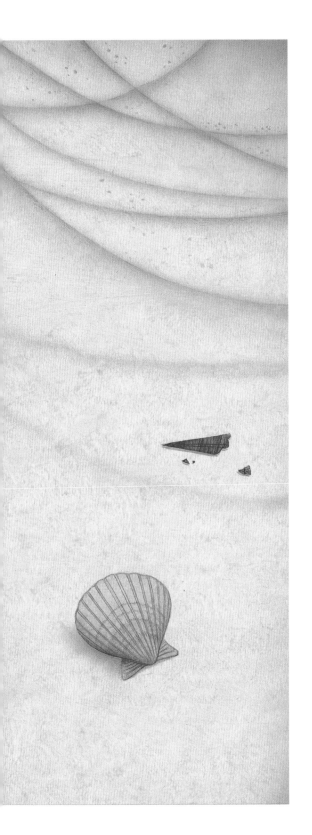

The rays of the morning sun
find my treasures spread out
for all to see.
I leave beautiful shells
and bits of coral
and pieces of wood with barnacles,
and high on the beach,
a line of foam dries in the breeze.

I am the ocean.

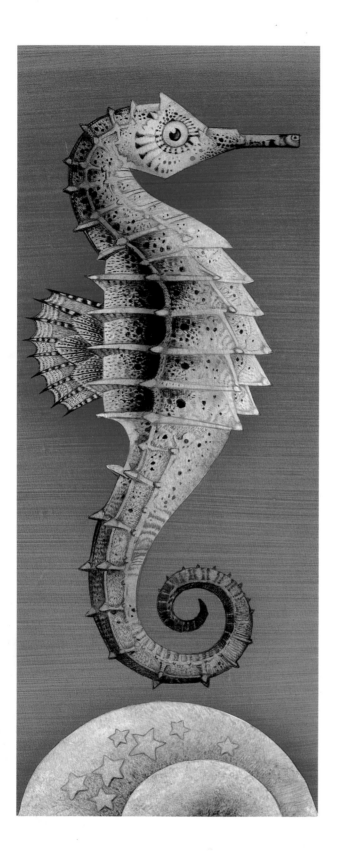

This book is dedicated
to the memory of my mother.—S.M.

Text copyright © 1991 by Suzanna Marshak
Illustrations copyright © 1991 by James Endicott

First Edition

Library of Congress Cataloging-in-Publication Data
Marshak, Suzanna.
    I am the ocean / by Suzanna Marshak ; illustrated
by James Endicott.
      p. cm.
    Summary: A lyrical paean to the ocean, in which
the ocean sings the song of itself and all it contains.
    ISBN 1-55970-065-3
    1. Ocean — Pictorial works — Juvenile
literature.   [1. Ocean.]   I. Endicott, James R.,
ill. II. Title.
GC21.5.M373 1991   90-27776
551.46 — dc20

Published in the United States by Arcade
Publishing, Inc., New York, a Little, Brown
company

Published simultaneously in Canada by Little,
Brown & Company (Canada) Limited

Designed by Marc Cheshire
Printed in Hong Kong
10 9 8 7 6 5 4 3 2 1